FOOTSTEPS
AROUND THE WORLD
Relocation Tips For Teens

San Diego Christian College
2100 Greenfield Drive
El Cajon, CA 92019

By Beverly D. Roman

Published by BR Anchor Publishing

ISBN 1-888891-35-1

Edited by Dalene R. Bickel

Research and contributions by
Amy L. Roman, MA, Counseling/Psychology

Book design and layout by Michael J. Cadieux. Michael is an award-winning graphics designer and an accomplished illustrator. His creative art has graced all of BR Anchor Publishing's books.

Footsteps Around the World is distributed by:
BR Anchor Publishing, 2044 Montrose Lane, Wilmington, NC 28405
Tel: + 910.256.9598, Fax: + 910.256.9579
Visit BR Anchor Publishing on the web: www.branchor.com

ORDERS
Call 1.800.727.7691 in the United States, + 910.256.9598 outside of the US or e-mail Amy Roman, Executive Director at aroman@branchor.com.

The text in framed boxes that appear throughout this book are from *The Gifted Kids Survival Guide: A Teen Handbook* by Judy Galbraith, M.A. and Jim Delisle, Ph.D., © 1996. Reprinted with permission of Free Spirit Publishing, Minneapolis, MN; 1.800.735.7323; www.freespirit.com

Acknowledgments

I would like to extend my most sincere appreciation
to the following people whose invaluable contributions
enhanced *Footsteps Around the World.*

Bernie Storie, Vice President for Enrollment, Moravian College, Bethlehem, PA, provides expertise about maximizing a college interview in "COLLEGE DISCUSSION TOPICS."

Matthew Neigh, Executive Director, Interaction International, Incorporated, details common misconceptions about international relocation and tells teens how they can create a positive experience in "MYTHS EXPOSED."

Dr. David Pollock, 1939-2004. David was co-founder of Interaction International, Incorporated. The chapter "EXIT RIGHT – ENTER RIGHT" discusses Dave's RAFT theory, which details why teens need to realize closure with their present friends before they can move on to relationships in their new community.

Emily Stocks, Raleigh, NC, critiqued *Footsteps Around the World* from a teenager's point of view. Her fresh perspective has been an asset and should benefit teens who read the book.

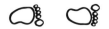

Follow Your Dreams

My "moving career" began with marriage to a Naval Officer who later worked for a company that also believed in frequent relocation. Moving every one to three years became a way of life for the Roman family and during all of our moves (18 total), I vowed to some day put pen to paper and write a book to help other relocating families. Using my own experience of how to find information about the new location and keep everything organized, I wrote my first manuscript, *Moving Minus Mishaps*. The next step was to get it published; but few publishers responded to my queries and none would accept my manuscript.

My determination to offer practical moving advice to relocating families led to self-publishing. I not only learned the publishing business, but also developed marketing strategies as well. I now own my own company, BR Anchor Publishing, and have written more than 20 books for adults, teenagers, preteens and young children that are sold all over the world.

If you have a special idea of something you wish to see become a reality, I encourage you to follow your dream as well. Good luck, and if you want to tell me your story, write to me at broman@branchor.com. I wish you all the best.

Beverly D. Roman

Contents
FOOTSTEPS AROUND THE WORLD

Section One
Relocation Basics

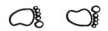

Section Two
International Moving

"They said it couldn't be done, but we did it."
—Anonymous

Section Three
Resources

1 Section One

is for teens who are moving across the street, across the state or around the world.

2 Section Two

continues the relocation journey with specifics for teens who are moving to another country.

3 Section Three

offers resources to learn about your new home and stay in touch with friends.

- three word games on pages 18, 45 and 81
- ✔ international road sign match on page 70
- a fun customs and manners quiz on page 71

Section One

Relocation Basics

1

Ten Tips For Talking To Parents

1. Choose your time wisely.
2. Be respectful.
3. Speak precisely and concisely.
4. When you talk to your parents about a problem, come prepared with suggestions for solving it.
5. Make a genuine effort to see their point.
6. Watch your body language.
7. Keep your voice down.
8. Avoid "you" statements such as "You don't understand me."
9. Pay attention.
10. Be willing to compromise. (Give a little and you might gain a lot.)

The text above is one of several quotations that will appear in this book. See page two for attribution.

Does Anyone Care About My Feelings?

My family and I have moved eighteen times domestically and internationally. Although I never moved when I was your age, I made these moves with three children and therefore, I believe I can empathize with you and offer worthwhile suggestions for your new venture.

During our many relocations, my children had their share of challenges. All of them experienced leaving friends, changing schools and reevaluating coveted sports positions and various hard-earned opportunities. Their emotions ranged from anger and sadness to relief (depending on the situation). They were encouraged to discuss their feelings and as a family, we found ways to discover the positive aspects about our moves. Years later, my children came to cherish their experiences and consider their moves as educational and maturing. As a result, they interface more easily with others and have developed more tolerance and understanding toward different peoples and cultures.

Get Proactive!

If you are feeling angry, sad or uncertain, these emotions are understandable, but these feelings need to be expressed and dealt with so that you can enjoy and benefit from your new location. Easy to say, but how can you keep from feeling like your world is coming to an end? *Get proactive!*

❒ Establish lines of communication.

❒ Learn about your new home (see page 17).

❒ Manage your move (see page 19).

❒ Reach out to help the rest of the family.

To establish lines of communication, I suggest having weekly family meetings with the goal being to help each other recognize the positive aspects about the move. Be careful not to let these get-togethers become "gripe" sessions. Believe it or not, your relocation will undoubtedly benefit your family in a variety of ways and—it may even become one of your most valuable experiences.

Reach out to help others, such as a younger brother or sister.

11

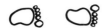

You can help them to learn about your new home and/or assist them in packing and organizing their belongings. Your contribution will not only benefit your siblings, but it will allow you to feel better because you will be doing something productive.

KEEP OLD FRIENDS

Before you leave, be sure to tell friends how important they are to you! You can maintain long-distance friendships by swapping photos, memories and notes, as well as home and e-mail addresses so you can continue to share important experiences.

If you have one special friend, think about exchanging a memento or personal gift with him or her. Having something special to remind you of each other will be very meaningful.

If the distance is not too great, discuss with your family the possibility of exchange visits with friends during vacations or long weekends. It's nice to keep old friends even though you meet new people. Who knows. You may move back to the same community in a few years!

BEGIN THE ADVENTURE

We are the sum total of our heritage and our experiences. The opportunity to learn about different cities, states, countries, people and cultures can be a chance to expand one's horizons. Changing homes and schools are not easy tasks, but they can be managed.

Most of the negative aspects of moving result from a lack of preparation and information. Therefore, use *Footsteps Around the World* as a tool to help you manage your move, learn about your new location and enhance your experience. Whether you are moving across town or across the globe, the knowledge you will attain from this book about yourself and your new community will help you to settle in and take advantage of the opportunities that await you.

Journaling

If you have never tried it, consider writing a personal journal about friends and places you want to remember. By recording your thoughts, feelings, experiences, goals, disappointments and dreams, "journaling" is an excellent way for you to get to know yourself better and think about what you want to accomplish in life. It will be fun to reread these entries years after you write them.

Keeping a personal journal will also help you to more effectively

- focus on what is really important in your life,
- explore creative writing,
- deal with problems that are troubling you,
- record memories and special events in your life,
- have a book for future reflection.

You can also form a small writing group with several friends and meet on a regular basis to talk over mutual challenges as well as write about them.

Fill out the personal profile on the right to help you keep all your pertinent data in one place.

Getting Started In Setting Your Goals
You'll need four things:
- a period of uninterrupted quiet time.
- a place where you can think and work comfortably.
- something to write with.
- something to write in or on.

Personal Profile

Name _____

New Address _____

_____

_____

Birth date _____ Birth place _____

Citizenship _____

Social Security number _____

Military I.D. number/tag _____

Driver's license number _____ Expires _____

Parents/guardian _____

_____

Brothers/sisters _____

_____

_____

CHURCH AFFILIATION

Special events (i.e., baptism, bar mitzvah) _____

_____

_____

_____

MEDICAL CHECKLIST

Blood type _____

Allergies _____

Medication _____

Dosage _____

Side effects _____

_____

Changing Addresses

Magazines   Date notified

_____   _____

_____   _____

_____   _____

_____   _____

_____

Music clubs   Date notified

_____   _____

_____   _____

_____   _____

_____   _____

_____

                                                        Date notified

Car registration   ☐ _____

Bank   ☐ _____

Car loan   ☐ _____

Credit card   ☐ _____

Other   ☐ _____

_____   ☐ _____

_____   ☐ _____

_____   ☐ _____

_____   ☐ _____

What Will Your New Home Be Like?

The research you do before moving is important because it will help you to take the "unknowns" (city, home and school) and turn them into real places to which you can relate. The more you know about your new city, the faster you will be able to settle in and feel comfortable.

INFORMATION SOURCES

THE INTERNET On the World Wide Web you can learn almost anything about a city, including its culture, architecture, sports, schools and parks. If your home computer is not equipped with a modem, you can access the Internet at school, or in public or university libraries. To learn about your new city, search under its name and the state abbreviation (example: Erie, PA) for topics and places of interest. There are also resources to help you learn about a city in the INTERNET DIRECTORY.

BOOKSTORES AND PUBLIC OR UNIVERSITY LIBRARIES The travel sections have maps and books about cities and countries to purchase or borrow.

CITY RESIDENTS Your family may have friends or colleagues in the community to which you are moving who can send information about areas that interest you.

VISITOR CENTERS OR CHAMBERS OF COMMERCE These offices provide information packets with an excellent overview of the city.

BROCHURES AND PHOTOGRAPHS Your family will be interfacing with movers and real estate agents who will provide pamphlets about highlights and places of interest in your new city. Your parents can also take pictures during their househunting trips of schools and areas that are important to you. If you have the opportunity to accompany them on a househunting trip, take advantage of it. Getting to see the city, the schools and meet teachers will remove some of the mystique of the new area.

> *"We are always equal to what we undertake with resolution."*
> **—Thomas Jefferson**

Seek-a-Word Puzzle

See if you can find the words listed below that relate to managing your move.

belongings	charity	cleaning
closets	clothing	donated
drawers	equipment	games
label	organize	pack
schedule	treasures	unbreakable
yard sale	relocation	moved

```
D C J Q U N B R E A K A B L E
A G G U Z T E Q U I P M E N T
Y A R D S A L E B A L H E R G
P M Q M R T O G N I N A E L C
G E O R G A N I Z E U A Q O I
P S M H D I G A T L S H I K C
W A F B H Y I S U U Z V U D H
T A V T M P N H R D W D N E M
T F O J T T G E B E C J H T U
C L O S E T S J O H W S M A M
C T R Q J M J P A C K A Z N C
B W C H O C Q R K S G O R O Q
H X Z V F H I K W Z E I L D G
Q L E G C T E T N Y T K J C Q
J D R V Y N O I T A C O L E R
```

18

Managing Your Move

One of the best ways to manage any stressful event such as a relocation is to gain control of your situation. There are some aspects about your move that you can't control (i.e., the timing or the city to which you are relocating), but there are certainly some that you can. Let's talk about what you should be able to manage and how to do it.

GET ORGANIZED

Organize your move schedule and your personal belongings. It will help you and your family if you develop lists of things you need to do for your move and plan a practical time frame in which to accomplish them.

Begin by cleaning out your closets and drawers. Outgrown clothing, games and items that you no longer use can be donated to a charitable organization, contributed to a yard sale (if your family has time to plan one) or given to a younger brother, sister, cousin or friend. You could also earn some spending money by selling items to a consignment or thrift shop. However, keep anything that you are undecided about. Don't ever throw away treasures when you are unsure of your feelings. After you have sorted through your belongings, pack and label unbreakable items that you want to be moved to your new home.

This is also a good time to locate important records and effects.

ITEM	LOCATION
❏ birth certificate	_____
❏ Social Security card	_____
❏ collectibles (cards/stamps/coins)	_____
❏ licenses and registration	_____
❏ passport	_____

Note: Be careful with your passport. Every year millions of passports are stolen, altered and used to commit crimes or to gain illegal entry into another country.

On the following pages, there are suggested moving tasks that you can complete in a four-week time frame. Follow your schedule because procrastination can lead to stressful feelings and make it harder to enjoy the last few weeks with your friends. Divide the tasks you need to accomplish and list them in "COMPLETING TASKS TIMETABLE" on pages 24-25.

CREATE YOUR OWN SPACE

If you have outgrown your bedroom decor, here is a chance to change it. As you plan your new room, consider using memorabilia from your friends and school as a pleasant reminder of your former home, as well as touches of the new city's highlights, school colors, and/or activities and sports. You can also be creative and plan a whole new look and color scheme for your space. Changing room decor does not have to be expensive. The goal is to make the room reflect you and your favorite things. If you have a computer, ask permission to have a modem line installed at your new home.

VISUALIZE A GOOD MOVE

Imagine yourself in a successful setting in your new town and school. Concentrate on ways you can fit in at the new school instead of worrying about whether or not you will be accepted. Your favorite pastimes, sports involvements and school activities will all lead to ways you can integrate into the school and develop new friendships.

And—add up your assets! Think about your personal achievements such as grades, awards and/or commendations, and how you were able to make friends in the past. Reviewing your successes will help you to develop a positive outlook, calm your fears and make your goals become a reality.

Completing Tasks Timetable

This four-week schedule suggests activities to help you organize your move in a logical time frame. If a moving company will be transporting your family's possessions, any breakable items should definitely be packed by the movers. However, you may want to pack other items yourself. Movers generally mark boxes by room name and label items such as "dresser contents." If you have books or items that you will want to locate upon arrival, you can pack them yourself and label them with specifics such as "gym gear" or "computer cords and attachments" on the outside of the box for quick access.

Four weeks

❒ Obtain W-2 forms from a previous employer, if applicable.

❒ Notify your teachers and school administration that you are moving. (You will need descriptions of your courses and curriculum and copies of grades.)

❒ Discard old papers or outdated materials.

❒ Create a file of important items that you will need to take with you, i.e., school and medical records and references from previous employers or volunteer organizations.

❒ Locate original boxes for equipment such as computers and stereos. If you no longer have them, check with office supply stores and bookstores for used, clean boxes.

❒ Go through your closets and drawers for outgrown clothing or items you no longer use.

❒ Think about starting a journal.

❒ Take pictures of friends and start a scrapbook.

Three weeks

❒ Give your new telephone number, address and e-mail to your friends.

❒ Draw a diagram of your new room using a scale of 1/4 inch = 1 foot. Then measure your furniture (height, depth and width) using the same scale and draw the furniture on the diagram. Rearrange as necessary to maximize your space.

21

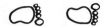

❏ Plan farewell parties and visits.

❏ Make a list of your personal belongings. (If you have never moved, or have not moved for a few years, you will be surprised at all you have accumulated. List all your belongings and give a copy of the list to a parent.)

❏ If you have an automobile, update the insurance coverage and make arrangements to have it serviced before you move.

See also "DRIVING PRIVILEGES" on page 44.

Two weeks

❏ Pick up items at the film processor or any other services.

❏ Pack a telephone directory of your current city.

❏ Pack items you do not use daily. (Wrap very small items in colored paper to avoid overlooking them when unpacking.)

❏ Label boxes you don't want packed by the mover with "DO NOT PACK" signs.

❏ Get involved with your family's travel plans. If time permits, your family may be able to combine the relocation trip to your new home with visits to new sites and/or cities.

❏ Collect friends' autographs. Space is reserved on the last two pages in this book for friends' signatures.

❏ Help your family with their "to do" lists.

❏ Arrange for your pet's care and traveling needs.

One week

❏ Check all the last-minute details on your lists.

❏ Clean out your school hall and gym lockers.

❏ Return and/or reclaim borrowed items such as library books, computer disks, athletic equipment or musical instruments.

> *"I don't know the key to success, but the key to failure is trying to please everybody."*
> **—Bill Cosby**

❏ Back up your computer files onto disks. Remove disks from the external drive and check your manual for the procedure to pack your computer to prevent component damage.

❏ Color code and/or mark all computer cords for easy reassembly.

❏ Make a list of food or snacks to pack if you will be traveling by car to your new home.

❏ Plan pastimes or activities for your trip. Consider items that will be good for long trips and do not take up much space.

❏ Prepare a list of necessities to take with you. Include this book!

❏ Pack and label items such as school materials if you will need them soon after arrival.

❏ When the movers finish packing your room, check the closets and permanent cabinet drawers to be sure no articles have been missed.

Write down your tasks on the next two pages.

23

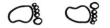

FOOTSTEPS AROUND THE WORLD

Things to do as soon as possible

Task   Date completed

_____   _____

_____   _____

_____   _____

_____   _____

_____   _____

_____   _____

_____   _____

_____   _____

_____   _____

Things to do by (date) _____

Task   Date completed

_____   _____

_____   _____

_____   _____

_____   _____

_____   _____

_____   _____

THINGS TO DO BY (DATE) _____

Task   Date completed

_____   _____

_____   _____

_____   _____

_____   _____

_____   _____

THINGS TO DO JUST BEFORE WE MOVE

Task   Date completed

_____   _____

_____   _____

_____   _____

_____   _____

_____   _____

_____   _____

_____   _____

_____   _____

_____   _____

_____   _____

_____   _____

_____   _____

Notes

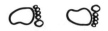

By now you have probably moved more times than you care to remember. Therefore, moving should be easy, right? You've been there, done that—no problem. However, saying good-bye to friends and/or family is always difficult.

Be sure to gather e-mail addresses before you move (there is space to list them in this book). Then no matter what city you move to, or even how many times you move in the future, you can instantly contact friends around the world for the price of a local phone call. Of course, traditional letters and occasional long distance calls help bridge the gap too. And—don't rule out seeing your friends again. Occasionally, military teens move to another base only to discover that an old friend has PCSd there as well!

When it comes to making new friends, recognize that you are not alone as there are approximately 400,000 US military teens. That means that no matter what installation you call home, a number of people your age will be there sharing the same experience. The key is to make an effort to meet them. You might not have to look far.

What Can You Find on Base?

Many bases have established youth sponsorship programs which pair relocating teens with teens at the new installation. This not only provides incoming teens with a source of information, it also offers an instant friend upon arrival. Ask your parents to request youth sponsorship information from their relocation managers before your move. Also, don't hesitate to visit the relocation center on your own if you have a particular question relating to your move.

Learn as much as possible about your new post, school and civilian community through the Internet. SITES has comprehensive information about your base. You can find this and other military websites in the INTERNET DIRECTORY. Be sure to find out if a curfew is observed. If so, you will only be able to exceed curfew

hours with proof of employment or a permission slip from your parents to attend a special event.

Once at the new installation, visit the Youth Services Center. Most military bases now feature teen programs and many offer a place for teens to get together after school. These facilities often provide sports equipment, recreational activities, a teen lounge and sometimes computers for Internet access. You might also consider joining or forming a teen council that produces information such as brochures for newcomers or a website about the installation. Additional places to meet other teens would be the local Armed Services YMCA, church youth groups and of course your school's extracurricular organizations.

Moving to a new community may involve a change in the cost of living. Prices for most necessities, including food, clothing, gasoline and entertainment, could be priced higher or lower than what you are accustomed to paying. This is just one of the many reasons why you need to manage your money wisely. When you become familiar with the costs in the next city, you can prepare a budget for yourself. Write down the purchases that are absolutely necessary and for which you are responsible. When you receive your allowance or a paycheck, set aside what you will need for required purchases. Before you have a chance to "impulse buy," try to put aside some monies for emergencies, especially if you are maintaining a car. Here are a few other financial tips to guide you.

BE AN EDUCATED CONSUMER

It's never too early to become an educated buyer. Know how to

- protect yourself from scams,
- comparison shop,
- request refunds for merchandise,
- carefully evaluate your purchases.

Several resources are listed in the INTERNET DIRECTORY to help you with these issues. One in particular is "CONSUMER EDUCATION FOR TEENS" listed under FINANCES which details everything from learning how to avoid being a victim of fraud to setting goals for your personal finances.

BANKING CHECKLIST

If you have your own banking account, you may have to locate another bank when you move. By transferring your account to a local bank, you can usually avoid the fees charged to access funds through an ATM (Automated Teller Machine).

If you are establishing an account for the first time, understand the responsibility that is involved. The websites in the INTERNET DIRECTORY also offer financial information for teens.

Here are some points for you and your parents to evaluate when selecting a bank.

CONSIDERATIONS

- fees for account maintenance
- automatic deposit system
- convenient ATM locations and withdrawal limits
- savings programs
- affiliations with international services
- free checking, interest checking and safety deposit boxes

MONEY TIPS FOR TRAVELERS

- ❐ Carry your money separately from your identification. If you are robbed, you will not lose both. Keep enough money for cab fare in a separate pocket.

- ❐ When you use Traveler's Checks, list the numbers and keep them separate from the checks in case of loss.

- ❐ Photocopy your credit card, identification and travel documents and leave a copy in a safe place.

MONEY TIPS FOR TRAVELERS is reprinted with permission from *Overseas Digest*, a free monthly online publication.

"Wisdom begins in wonder."
— **Socrates**

Evaluating Schools

Whatever school you are considering, it's essential that you and your family evaluate the courses and the environment. Discuss any questions or concerns with your parents and ask them to check on these during their homefinding visit. You need to understand the school's academic requirements and social atmosphere, as well as its rules and regulations. Your research will help to assure that you become comfortable in the new school and successfully matriculate into the academic programs.

CHECKLIST FOR A NEW SCHOOL

- ❐ a favorable accreditation rating
- ❐ a well-stocked library with up-to-date books
- ❐ classroom computers and strong focus on modern technology
- ❐ required courses
- ❐ adequate instruction of foreign languages
- ❐ the school's profile (standardized test scores, university placements and national enrollments)
- ❐ provisions for academic and non-academic needs
- ❐ services for special needs
- ❐ theater, creative groups and school newspapers
- ❐ sports and activities that you enjoy

Seniors Choosing Not to Move

If you are in eleventh or twelfth grade, you may be undecided about completing your final high school year at your present school or moving with your family and attending a new school. To help you make this difficult decision, I recommend that you outline your options, evaluate both situations and then realistically analyze your choices with your family. Write down the pros and cons of everything that is important to you and be very honest with yourself as you weigh your alternatives.

Even though it is hard to leave a school as a senior, there are advantages to moving with your family. Most important is that your senior year is the last block of time that you will have with your family before you leave for college. You will also have the opportunity to experience another part of the country and meet people whom you otherwise would never have known.

If you choose to remain in your present community, and if your family supports your decision, recognize that frequent contact and communication must be maintained.

Issues to discuss

☐ expenditure limitations and methods to access funds

☐ procedures and contacts for medical care

☐ how you and your family will communicate for routine and emergency issues

☐ how to place calls for police, fire and ambulance services

☐ how frequently you will see one another

☐ your host family's expectations

☐ your curfew guidelines

☐ your school responsibilities

☐ car and travel privileges

If you will remain in your present city, you, your family and your host family all need to understand and agree on these basic issues, as well as any others that are relevant to your situation.

Tips For Talking To Teachers

✎ Make an appointment to meet and talk.

✎ Think through what you want to say before your meeting.

✎ Choose your words carefully.

✎ Don't expect the teacher to do all the work or propose all the answers.

✎ Be diplomatic, tactful and respectful.

✎ Focus on what you need, not on what you think the teacher is doing wrong.

✎ Don't forget to listen.

✎ Bring your sense of humor.

✎ If your meeting is not successful, get help from another adult.

Schools Attended

School attended	From/To	Credits

Training/Skills

_____

_____

_____

_____

Awards/Commendations

_____

_____

_____

_____

Transcripts/Certificates

_____

_____

_____

Comments

_____

_____

_____

My Sports

SPORTS I AM TAKING PART IN NOW

MY COACH

_____
_____
_____
_____

SPORTS I WANT TO PURSUE IN MY NEW CITY

_____
_____
_____
_____

_____
_____
_____
_____

NEW SKILLS TO LEARN

DATE

_____
_____
_____
_____

_____
_____
_____
_____

Friends to Remember

NAME _____

Address _____

_____

Tel _____ E-mail _____

What I remember most _____

_____

NAME _____

Address _____

_____

Tel _____ E-mail _____

What I remember most _____

_____

NAME _____

Address _____

_____

Tel _____ E-mail _____

What I remember most _____

_____

NAME _____

Address _____

_____

Tel _____ E-mail _____

What I remember most _____

_____

You may photocopy this page.

Friends to Remember

NAME _____

Address _____

_____

Tel _____ E-mail _____

What I remember most _____

_____

NAME _____

Address _____

_____

Tel _____ E-mail _____

What I remember most _____

_____

KEEP IN TOUCH

It's fun sending and receiving e-mails, but you can also chat live around the world at www.branchor.com/chat.htm. BR Anchor Publishing provides a secure online chat room that you can use with your friends and family through your local Internet service.

SCRAPBOOKS

A really nice way to remember your friends, home and city is to create a scrapbook. Scrapbooks are not only fun to make, but they are a way for you to preserve your memories, as well as connect your old and new friends. Years from now you will have fun reminiscing about people you knew and places you visited, and you will laugh about the funny hair and clothing styles you once wore.

37

Dating Tips

If you currently have a boyfriend/girlfriend, you are understandably upset about moving to a new city. Regardless of how long you have been dating this individual, it will be difficult to say good-bye. Whether or not you wish to continue this relationship via e-mail and telephone conversations is a decision only you can make.

However, if you do not have a special friend, moving to a new location might be a great opportunity to meet someone (provided, of course, your parents agree that you are old enough to date). This individual need not be handsome, beautiful or a star athlete, but simply someone who is truly interested in what you have to say, respects you, is honest, is fun to be with and enjoys life.

If someone in your neighborhood or school has caught your attention, you might want to invite him or her on a date. Depending on your age, driving ability, curfew and comfort level, you can go out as a group, plan a party or spend an afternoon/evening together in a public place.

Plan Ahead

Have something in mind when you ask a person for a date. Some types of dates require more conversation than others, such as a movie versus a dinner. So decide how comfortable you would be in the situation you are considering.

Typical dating activities
- bowling
- roller blading/ice skating
- miniature golf
- hiking/biking
- museums or historical sites
- walking tours
- sporting events
- dances
- amusement parks

39

🏃 shopping
🏃 picnics

The two of you could also volunteer your time, such as take part in charity walks/runs, visit a sick friend or join a group building a home for Habitat for Humanity.

Special events can be found in the local newspaper or you can pick up information packets about things to do in your city at the visitor center or Chamber of Commerce.

Safety Precautions

Whether dating or traveling alone, always follow these safety tips.

❏ Be aware of your surroundings and the routes you take when traveling to a function or activity.

❏ Note telephone locations (or carry a cellular phone).

❏ Memorize landmarks and keep to well-lit areas.

❏ Always tell a parent/guardian who you will be with, where you are going and what time you will return.

❏ Limit how much personal information you give to new acquaintances.

❏ Listen to your head rather than your heart.

❏ Ask a trusted friend or an adult for advice if you are confused about a situation.

❏ Always meet in a public place.

❏ Do not go anywhere with someone until you get to know them.

❏ Heed your instincts. If a situation makes you uncomfortable, contact a friend or parent.

❏ Take your time!

Interview preparation is not necessarily a relocation issue; however, you could be applying for part-time employment or anticipating college interviews. This section contains sample questions for both situations. If you are preparing for your first interview, I suggest that you practice answering the questions listed below with someone before your meeting. Even though you may feel nervous at the outset, the practice will help you to feel more relaxed and at ease during your interview.

DO'S AND DON'TS

Arrange for an interview by letter or by telephone. Write down the date, time, name and title of the interviewer (correctly spelled), telephone number and directions to the facility. Allow enough time for travel so that you are punctual for your meeting (fifteen minutes early is recommended). Call ahead if a delay is unavoidable.

Appropriate interview clothing is conservative. Do not take a friend with you to the interview and do not smoke. Do not use excessive hand gestures or frown. Introduce yourself, shake hands firmly and remain standing until you are offered a seat. Be sure to maintain eye contact and use proper grammar.

Be courteous and sincere and let the interviewer direct the conversation. Listen carefully to learn as much as possible about the position or the school. Request to see the department and meet the people where you could be working or studying.

EMPLOYMENT DISCUSSION TOPICS

QUESTIONS YOU MAY ENCOUNTER IN AN INTERVIEW:

- Why are you interested in this type of job?
- Why did you choose this company?
- Do you think your grades are a good indication of your achievement at school?
- What are your weaknesses? *Prepare a response to this question and mention how you plan to rectify the situation.*

Example: improve typing skills by taking a course.

? What are your greatest strengths?

? What do you think you will gain from this company?

? What can you contribute to this company and why should we hire you?

? What salary are you expecting? *Respond by asking what they are offering or what the previous employee was paid.*

QUESTIONS YOU SHOULD ASK:

? What will my responsibilities be?

? How many hours a week will I be working?

? What are some of the more difficult challenges of this job?

? What type of notice do you require if my school assignments interfere with my work schedule?

? To what extent will I be working independently or as a team member?

? Could this position become full-time after graduation?

? If salary has not been mentioned, ask what the job will pay.

COLLEGE DISCUSSION TOPICS
By Bernie Storie, Vice President for Enrollment,
Moravian College, Bethlehem, Pennsylvania

QUESTIONS YOU MAY ENCOUNTER IN AN INTERVIEW:

? What college characteristics have you identified as being most important in your college search?

? What has been your strategy to find the right college?

? What course or courses have you most enjoyed over your high school career?

? Can you describe your study habits for me?

? What will I learn about you when I read your application for admission? Or, how will your application stand out?

- What would your teachers say are your greatest strengths as a student? As a person?
- What will be "The Good Life" for you twenty years from now?
- What bothers you most about the world around you?
- Tell me about your family. What do you expect you will miss most about your family when you enroll in college?

QUESTIONS YOU SHOULD ASK:

- In addition to my grades and test scores, what information will you use to assess my application?
- On what basis is the faculty of this college rewarded?
- What is the average class size?
- What percentage of freshmen come back for their sophomore year?
- What are the greatest strengths of this college? Its weaknesses?
- How many students from my hometown are enrolled here?
- To what other colleges do most of your applicants also apply for admission?
- What is the endowment per student at this college?

FINAL SUGGESTIONS

Don't be afraid to request a moment to think about an answer to a question. If you are asked an obviously improper question, ask how that question will be pertinent to the job or your school application. If you have any sensitive areas that might be brought up in the interview, think about plausible responses before the interview begins.

Before the interview ends, look for an opportunity to summarize your two or three best qualifications. Ask when you will be notified of their decision or if you should follow up with a telephone call. Finish with a positive comment and express your interest in the position or the college. *Always* follow up with a thank you note that has been checked for spelling and grammar.

Driving Privileges

A fun double puzzle with the capitalized words in this paragraph is on the next page. If you will be moving out-of-state, you may need to take a TEST to obtain a new driver's LICENSE. Understand the state LAWS, TRAFFIC LIGHTS, STOP SIGNS and all ROAD SIGNS. Obtain INSURANCE coverage and REGISTRATION and use DEFENSIVE driving techniques. If you own or have access to a car, know its MODEL and YEAR, and routinely have it checked by a MECHANIC. Check the MILEAGE before your car is SERVICED, the TIRES ROTATED and the OIL FILTER is changed.

Name _____

Address _____

_____

Insurance _____

Contact _____

Tel _____Fax _____ E-mail_____

Name that appears on title _____

Registration # _____License # _____

Model _____Year _____

Notes _____

_____

MAINTENANCE RECORD

service center _____ phone _____

car mileage _____ date _____

tire rotation _____ date _____

oil/filter change_____ date _____

other _____ date _____

_____ date _____

_____ date _____

Double Puzzle

Unscramble the words below that relate to driving privileges. Then match the numbered letters to discover the secret driving phrase. The answers are on page 92.

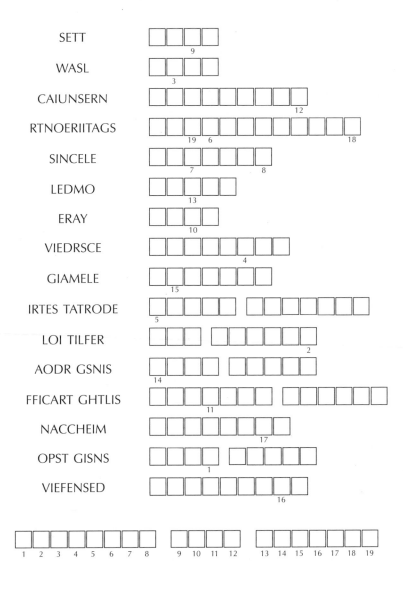

SETT

WASL

CAIUNSERN

RTNOERIITAGS

SINCELE

LEDMO

ERAY

VIEDRSCE

GIAMELE

IRTES TATRODE

LOI TILFER

AODR GSNIS

FFICART GHTLIS

NACCHEIM

OPST GISNS

VIEFENSED

1 2 3 4 5 6 7 8   9 10 11 12   13 14 15 16 17 18 19

45

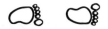

Travel Diary

Moved from _____

To _____ Dates _____

Our itinerary included:

_____

_____

_____

Fun things we did on our trip_____

_____

_____

_____

_____

Places we saw _____

_____

_____

_____

_____

People we met_____

_____

_____

_____

_____

What I most enjoyed and why _____

_____

_____

_____

_____

We've Arrived–Now What?

Keep things in perspective! There are good and not-so-good aspects to every place you live. If you really think about it, there are probably reasons why you were glad to leave your last home and school. No matter where you are living, it is important that you be happy and make the most of your experience.

Continue the family meetings I suggested in the beginning of the book. During these meetings try to focus on at least one good episode that occurred the previous week. Be patient with yourself if you do not feel as though you are adjusting as fast as your siblings or the rest of your family. Everyone accepts changes in different ways and at different speeds. As time goes on, you will be surprised to learn that you have more accomplishments and fewer concerns. That is when you will know you are comfortable with your new home!

Tried and True Tips to Settle In

❐ Don't get behind in school! If you are struggling with a subject or activity, seek help from your teacher, parent or school counselor as soon as possible.

❐ Learn something new about your city at every opportunity.

❐ Go exploring. Check out theme parks, museums or whatever your city has to offer.

❐ Volunteer your time to a charitable organization.

❐ Join clubs with your favorite activities.

❐ Write and send photographs about your town to friends and ask them to send you recent photos as well.

❐ Reach out to make new friends.

❐ Know that if you feel sad, angry or upset, these feelings are caused by the *change*—not by the people or the place.

❐ Maintain traditions, dinners and/or celebrations that are special to your family to help you preserve your heritage.

❐ Take one day at a time.

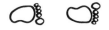

CELEBRATIONS I WANT TO KEEP:

_____

_____

_____

_____

THINGS TO DO AND PLACES TO GO

- ❏ Visit your new school and meet your teachers.
- ❏ Try to meet new classmates and neighborhood friends.
- ❏ Learn your school's rules, regulations and hours.
- ❏ Apply for a new driver's license.
- ❏ Update your auto insurance information in the appropriate time frame (often 30 days).
- ❏ Locate the extracurricular activities that you enjoy.

Getting involved in school teams and community activities will allow you to meet people in smaller groups. It is usually easier to begin a conversation with others who have interests and goals that are similar to yours.

SAFETY TIPS

- ❏ Learn the neighborhoods that are considered safe.
- ❏ Use well-traveled routes when you are in a new part of the city or country.
- ❏ Do not draw attention to yourself in unfamiliar places.
- ❏ Have a reliable backup contact telephone number in case you cannot reach someone in your family.
- ❏ Know the street names surrounding your home.
- ❏ Memorize telephone numbers and street addresses for home and parents' place of work.
- ❏ Lock all doors when the family is absent from your home and use the alarm system if you have one.
- ❏ Plan practice routes to exit your home in case of fire.

❒ Be sure there is a locking bar on all sliding glass doors.

❒ Do not hide keys outside of your home.

❒ Do not leave notes outside of your home indicating that you are away.

❒ Learn emergency telephone numbers for fire, ambulance and police if 911 is not available in your community.

CULTURAL CHANGE

Moving to a new location affects some people more profoundly than others. If you suddenly develop feelings of sadness, anger or frustration for no apparent reason, you may be experiencing cultural change, or what is commonly referred to as "culture shock." Although this condition is generally associated with international moves, an often overlooked reality is that moving within and around a country (such as from a large metropolis to a rural community) can trigger this reaction as well.

Earlier in this book I suggested ways that you can research a city before you move. Learning about the city's highlights, architecture, ethnic groups, sports teams and customs and dialects will help you to feel more comfortable once you arrive. Preparation isn't the complete solution to preventing culture shock, but it can go a long way toward minimizing its effects.

Even if you are so excited about your move that you can hardly stand it, you may still experience culture shock after you have been living in unfamiliar surroundings for awhile. Fortunately, the condition is not permanent! Time, involvement and becoming acclimated and comfortable in your new community will all combine to help you transcend this experience.

☞ **RECOGNIZE THAT YOU ARE UNIQUE.** Do not compare yourself to anyone; believe that you are good enough to stand on your own merits.

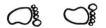

Welcome Clubs

Some schools have an organization or a "Welcome Club" that helps new students or incoming freshmen become acclimated by providing them with a way to meet people and become involved in activities. If such an organization does not exist at your school, talk to a teacher or counselor about establishing one.

In addition to the following suggestions, think about what you would most appreciate as an incoming student and incorporate those ideas into your school's organization.

❏ Obtain lists of incoming students from the school office or school counselor.

❏ Write to the students before they arrive to let them know about the program.

❏ Prepare a brochure about the school and the community.

❏ Assign students to be responsible for new students' orientation.

❏ Welcome new students upon their arrival.

❏ Learn about newcomers' special interests and activities and help them register.

❏ Create ways for newcomers to meet students and teachers.

❏ Inform new students about the local customs, sayings, pastimes and activities.

❏ Maintain contact with new students for at least one or two months.

❏ Invite new students to join the Welcome Club and ask them to share their experiences with others. Some students who have never moved may not realize what it is like to be a new student in a school.

One in six students moves every year, plus many schools have exchange students in their midst, so your efforts to establish a quality organization can benefit many teens.

> *"No one can make you feel inferior without your consent."*
> **—Eleanor Roosevelt**

You don't need me to tell you that there are huge challenges all over the world for young people today. And there are many theories about why someone takes a wrong turn in life, or becomes involved with undesirable people or activities. Every day, people (young and old) are subjected to books and entertainment that are not positive or healthy. In addition, teens like yourself who move often can experience the additional pressure of trying to "fit in" in different cultures and environments. One positive way to help you surmount challenges such as these is to choose wholesome pastimes and friends and become involved with worthwhile organizations.

Being able to make friends will help you adjust to a different school and feel comfortable in a new environment. The best advice I can offer you as you consider new acquaintances is—be selective. When in doubt, select strong friends, people who have values similar to yours. Learn as much as possible about a person or group at school or in your neighborhood before you get too close to them. It's important that you feel comfortable with the people you meet and the situations you encounter. And above all—be true to yourself. Don't let anyone talk you into anything that you don't want to do.

See TIPS TO BREAK THE ICE on the next page.

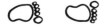

TIPS TO BREAK THE ICE

- Show an interest in other people. Don't expect people to automatically include you in their lives. Instead, you may have to make the effort to initiate a conversation.

- When you approach someone new, remember that people at any age like to feel as though others are interested in them.

- Begin a conversation by complimenting a classmate on something such as a good class presentation or the great game that they played the past weekend.

- Ask new acquaintances to tell you about themselves.

- Don't overdose new friends with stories about how wonderful your old school or city was, or about the amazing friends you had there.

- Intersperse your conversation with inquiries about your new community.

- Maintain a sense of humor.

- Try to keep a positive attitude, even when things don't go exactly your way.

- Be yourself!

If it is not easy for you to make new friends, there is some good advice at "SHYKIDS.COM" listed in our INTERNET DIRECTORY.

Friendship Versus Popularity

- Be content with one or two solid friendships; they're worth more than you realize.
- Don't expect everyone to like you. (Do you like everyone you meet?)
- Seek activities and groups that form around a common interest.
- Talk to your parents. Problems seem less daunting and more manageable if you share them.
- Be yourself. Friendships work best when they are based on honesty and sincerity.

Part-Time Jobs

Whether you are looking for a summer job or a part-time job during the school year, your value in the marketplace will be dictated by what you know, the demand for services and your reliability and experience. To find out what type of help is needed, and to equate a fee for your work, comparison shop classified advertisements in the Sunday newspaper or ask your friends what they charge for similar jobs. Consider employment that requires your skills and matches your personality and abilities. Whatever work you choose, take your responsibilities seriously and do not have friends visit you at work.

Typical part-time jobs:

- waitress/waiter
- bagging groceries
- lawn or yard care
- house painting
- vacation pet care
- newspaper delivery
- washing cars
- teaching people to use computers or the Internet
- errands or baking/cooking for busy or elderly people

Small businesses also benefit from reliable and mature part-time, minimum pay help. Even though the pay may be modest, you will gain skills, information and learn how to interface with adults in a work-related environment.

QUESTIONS TO ASK

- What will my responsibilities be?
- How many hours a week will I be working?
- What type of notice do you require if my school assignments interfere with my work schedule?
- If salary has not been mentioned, have an idea of what you expect to receive per hour, and when you will be paid.

BABY-SITTING GUIDE

 Meet with parents and children before accepting an assignment.

 Know the number of children and their ages.

 Know the names of everyone in the family.

 Discuss the required sitting time and your method of transportation to and from the home.

 Have a clear understanding of your responsibilities, the house rules and what the children may or may not do.

 Post these near the telephone:

   ✔ street address and telephone number where you are sitting;

   ✔ emergency telephone numbers for hospital, ambulance, poison control and police and fire departments;

   ✔ contact numbers for the parents and close neighbors.

 Make your priority caring for the children at all times.

See also "SAFE SITTER" in the INTERNET DIRECTORY with excellent safety tips for baby-sitters.

Meeting Challenges

These worksheets are to encourage you to develop productive ways to overcome challenging situations. Write down problems you are having, what caused them and what you did, or believe you can do, to feel better. If you discover patterns of behavior or feelings with which you are not pleased, talk with a trusted adult about ways to successfully meet your challenges.

FEELING/DATE _____

_____

Cause _____

I feel better by _____

_____

_____

_____

_____

FEELING/DATE _____

_____

Cause _____

I feel better by _____

_____

_____

_____

_____

Continued on the next three pages.

55

FOOTSTEPS AROUND THE WORLD

FEELING/DATE _____

_____

Cause _____

I feel better by _____

_____

_____

_____

_____

✎ **TAKE RESPONSIBILITY FOR THE STRESS YOU'RE EXPERIENCING.**
You control your perceptions and you are responsible
for your feelings. Other people can do or say things that
"trigger" certain feelings within you, but they don't make
you feel a certain way.

FEELING/DATE _____

_____

Cause _____

I feel better by _____

_____

_____

_____

_____

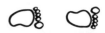

FEELING/DATE _____

_____

Cause _____

I feel better by _____

_____

_____

_____

_____

☞ **HANDLE STRESS.** Identify the specific aspects (people, events or circumstances) that you associate with feeling anxious or pressured.

☞ **TAKE POSITIVE ACTION.** Diminish or eliminate the problem, change your attitude toward the problem or engage in one or more stress-reducing activities.

FEELING/DATE _____

_____

Cause _____

I feel better by _____

_____

_____

_____

_____

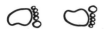

FOOTSTEPS AROUND THE WORLD

FEELING/DATE _____

_____

Cause _____

I feel better by _____

_____

_____

_____

_____

> ✆ **SHARE YOUR GOALS WITH A FRIEND.** Identify a support person and ask if he or she would be willing to hear about your goals and offer support and constructive criticism. Dreams become more real when you air them; problems more manageable when you share them; achievements more enjoyable when you have someone to celebrate with.

FEELING/DATE _____

_____

Cause _____

I feel better by _____

_____

_____

_____

_____

Help Yourself by Helping Others

How are you presently using your free time? Are you pleased with your activities? Your friends? Or, are you searching for something else in your life?

If you have time on your hands, think about volunteering your talent(s) to a local charity, community organization or a neighbor. By helping others you will ease lonely feelings, contribute to a community, develop a new perspective on life and meet interesting people. And—even though this isn't your primary goal, volunteering services will enhance your college applications.

It is important that you find a volunteer opportunity that fits your schedule, personality and skills. Local churches usually have need of volunteers, and most city newspapers list volunteer opportunities. Here are a few areas to consider.

- Special Olympics
- Habitat for Humanity
- Literacy programs
- Hospitals
- Libraries
- Elder care facilities
- Animal shelters
- American Red Cross
- Environmental organizations
- Scouting

There are numerous organizations with which you can become affiliated. Look around your neighborhood; there may be someone nearby who would welcome your assistance and/or companionship. Each time you use your gifts, and each time you reach out to enrich the lives of others, you are becoming a more successful person.

See also "VOLUNTEER EFFORTS" in the INTERNET DIRECTORY.

Section Two

International Moving

2

Question: What Do These Six Things Have In Common?

- ✐ cheese
- ✐ chocolate chip cookies
- ✐ Coca-Cola
- ✐ penicillin
- ✐ Post-It notes
- ✐ Silly Putty

Answer: All six were discovered or invented by mistake. According to Mark Twain, "accident" is the greatest inventor who ever lived. In *Mistakes That Worked,* author Charlotte F. Jones points out that accident (not necessity) is the mother of invention.

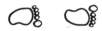

Myths Exposed *By Matthew Neigh*

So you are moving overseas! Moving to another country places a whole new perspective on relocation. It's important to realize that as a teenager your perspective and adjustment will be different not only from your parents, but from your siblings as well. Many teenagers like yourself have moved all over the world—some have had no problems while others have struggled. One of the differences between a good experience and a difficult one is whether you buy into any one of three myths about moving overseas.

MYTH 1: IF I CAN JUST STICK IT OUT FOR THE SHORT TIME I'M HERE

You may be headed to another country with the plan of simply "doing your time" and waiting until that glorious day when you can return "home" to your passport country. Instead, I suggest you take the time to enjoy this unique privilege by trying to understand and immerse yourself in the culture. Don't mock the culture or constantly compare it to your passport country.

Realize that what you are going to experience in your short time in a foreign culture is more than many people experience in a lifetime. I know that as a teenager in Europe, I didn't appreciate my experience. Unfortunately, it wasn't until years later that I developed an attitude of thankfulness for my heritage. By living abroad, you will have developed the skills and abilities necessary to a global workforce. But first you need to understand and appreciate the opportunity.

MYTH 2: THINGS CAN'T BE THAT DIFFERENT—THEY HAVE COKE, MCDONALDS AND MTV

Although your new country may appear to have some of the same name-brand products you are familiar with, you will discover that differences abound. For example, fast-food restaurants won't have outside pick-up windows and the popular music in your new country will probably be comprised of songs and artists you have never heard of before. You will undoubtedly notice other differences as well; perhaps you won't be eligible to drive for awhile because of different age limits,

but the extensive train/subway systems might compensate by making it easy to travel to the city or even to another country.

Talk with your family about what it is going to be like. Questions like, "Will I be able to drive?" "Will I have the same freedoms I have here at home?" can open up a dialogue between you and your dad and mom about what you can expect. Your family may not have all the answers, and that's okay. What is important is that all of you are sharing your expectations. No one likes surprises—especially when you are moving to a foreign country!

MYTH 3: EVERYTHING WILL BE THE SAME WHEN I GET BACK

You may falsely assume that you won't experience culture shock, or at least not struggle with it, and/or you may think that you won't change and that life as you currently know it won't change either. The truth is, we all are constantly changing. You will have changed after your short time abroad, the world back "home" will have changed and your friends will have changed—but not together. It's often tough to relate to your old friends and make new ones, even after only a year away.

Coming back, or repatriating, to your passport country *is* going to be different. Your best friends won't sit around every day for a year or two, awaiting your return. They may stay in touch, but they might also develop new friendships. Upon your return, it is going to require that *you* initiate friendships, whether old or new ones. You can do it! Having a proper perspective of what it is going to be like in another country is half the battle.

Matthew (Matt) Neigh is Executive Director of Interaction International, Incorporated, an organization that serves as a resource to the internationally mobile community. In that capacity, Matt has traveled to over 40 countries on every continent conducting pre-assignment and repatriation seminars and training for internationally mobile employees. Matt serves as president of Families in Global Transition and publishes Among Worlds *magazine. He shares knowledge and experiences from his personal journey growing up as a multilingual/multicultural expatriate kid in Europe, but also from years of being involved in the lives of expatriates of all ages, nationalities and backgrounds. Contact Matt at matthewneigh@interactionintl.org or 1.719.531.6181.*

Preparation and planning are the keys to help you feel comfortable in a new country much more quickly. Plan to learn as much as possible about the country before you move, and continue to make an effort to learn and understand the customs after you arrive. Perhaps some of your commonly accepted pastimes and activities will not be available, and these will have to be replaced with others more typical of the culture. Discuss these issues with your family and ask them to inquire about some of your interests during their premove visit(s) to the country.

FINDING THE FACTS

In addition to the Internet, public and university libraries and the American Automobile Association (for members) are sources to learn about a country. Most international moves are coordinated by major moving companies which offer packets of information about areas such as the time zones, climate, weather, currency, and housing and transportation options in your destination country. If your family has the opportunity to use relocation services abroad, these companies also have country-specific information. Read through any material your family acquires and search the INTERNET DIRECTORY in this book.

CURRENCY

Convert some home country funds into various denominations of the currency you will be using in your new country. Take the time to become familiar with the different denominations and the exchange rate. It is important that you are knowledgeable about the money and its value before you have to use it. If you are accustomed to using Automated Teller Machines (ATMs), know that ATMs in some countries will not accept a PIN (personal identification number) with more than four digits.

DRIVER'S LICENSE

If you are old enough to drive in the country to which you are moving, you can obtain an international driving permit by contacting the American Automobile Association (AAA).

International driving permits are valid for one year. Two passport photos are required and permits generally cost $10.00.

LANGUAGE AND CULTURE

Understanding and speaking the language is an important part of integrating into a country. It will help you feel comfortable in the environment and will be highly regarded in most countries. Think about it. If a student from another country moved to your school, you would probably expect this person to accept your way of life, understand your values and speak your language. It will be helpful to have a basic knowledge of the language before moving and then the means to learn more after your arrival. Some international schools provide language instruction, but if your school does not, find out what other resources are available.

CULTURAL DIFFERENCES

This topic was discussed on page 47 in "WE'VE ARRIVED— NOW WHAT?" for domestic moves. If you missed this section, take a few minutes now to read about culture shock and then return to this chapter. You should also understand the following:

- 👫 rules and regulations of your school and community,
- 👫 attitudes and attire that are acceptable or unacceptable,
- 👫 manners, expectations and social practices of the city and/or country.

Finally, venture out of your "comfort zone." For instance, instead of eating at a restaurant that you could find at home, visit local restaurants and try different foods. Attempting to integrate into the country's culture will be exciting and provide you with some treasured experiences.

See "CITY/COUNTRY INFORMATION" in the INTERNET DIRECTORY to find country-specific information.

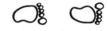

My New Country's Customs

Typical ways to greet people

_____

_____

_____

_____

Signs, gestures or comments that are typical in your country may be considered offensive in your new country. Some could be:

_____

_____

_____

_____

BASIC LANGUAGE PHRASES

My name is _____

Hello _____

Goodbye _____

Please _____

Thank you _____

Excuse me. _____

Help! _____

My telephone number is _____

My address is _____

Where is the bathroom? _____

Do you speak English? _____

I do not understand. _____

See "CITY/COUNTRY INFORMATION" in the INTERNET DIRECTORY to find country-specific information.

Foreign Phrases to Learn

These two worksheets will help you practice some more phrases in your new language. Spelling the words phonetically will help you to remember them easier.

My Language	New Language	Phonetic Spelling
_____	_____	_____
_____	_____	_____
_____	_____	_____
_____	_____	_____
_____	_____	_____
_____	_____	_____
_____	_____	_____
_____	_____	_____
_____	_____	_____
_____	_____	_____
_____	_____	_____
_____	_____	_____
_____	_____	_____
_____	_____	_____
_____	_____	_____
_____	_____	_____
_____	_____	_____
_____	_____	_____

Foreign Phrases to Learn

My Language	New Language	Phonetic Spelling
_____	_____	_____
_____	_____	_____
_____	_____	_____
_____	_____	_____
_____	_____	_____
_____	_____	_____
_____	_____	_____
_____	_____	_____
_____	_____	_____
_____	_____	_____
_____	_____	_____
_____	_____	_____
_____	_____	_____
_____	_____	_____
_____	_____	_____
_____	_____	_____
_____	_____	_____
_____	_____	_____
_____	_____	_____
_____	_____	_____
_____	_____	_____

International Road Signs

Can you guess what these symbols represent? If you need help, the answers are on page 92.

1   2   3

4   5   6

7   8   9

10   11   12

___ credit cards not accepted   ___ children at play

___ no fires allowed   ___ road narrows

___ gas and diesel station   ___ caution: bicycles

___ traffic circle area   ___ pedestrian crosswalk

___ slippery road ahead   ___ railroad crossing

___ no horseback riding   ___ biochemical hazard

Customs and Manners Quiz

IN THIS COUNTRY...

1. You should not place your hands in your pockets when speaking to someone.
2. To "queue up" is the proper way to wait in line.
3. Signal number one by holding your thumb upright.
4. People love to applaud. If you are applauded, be respectful and return the ovation.
5. Laughter and giggles may mean the listener is perplexed and unsure of what to say. (Try rephrasing your statement.)
6. Deference is shown to the elderly. (Don't be surprised if you are bypassed and they are waited on first.)
7. It is improper to show bare shoulders, stomach, calves or thighs.
8. Do not blink your eyes conspicuously when speaking with someone, as this is a sign of disrespect and boredom.
9. It is considered rude to leave the dinner table during a meal.
10. Do not wear shorts when visiting a church.
11. It is common to refuse an extra serving at least two times when dining. If you wish more, accept the third offer.
12. The handshake is still the common form of greeting.
13. Crossing your legs or putting your feet up on furniture may be seen as a sign of disrespect.
14. It is common for people to decline the gift several times before accepting it.
15. Showing anger is the worst way to achieve anything.
16. It is very rude to chew gum or use toothpicks in public.
17. Staring is quite common. Do not be offended if someone is staring at you.
18. Littering is strictly forbidden and subject to heavy fines.
19. Female visitors should be especially sensitive about making any glance or gesture that might be considered flirtatious.
20. You should almost always pay at the register, no tipping. Expect to hear diners "slurping" their noodles.

The answers are on page 92.

School Notes

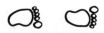

School evaluation needs to include the school's requirements, programs of study and activities or courses of interest to you. The credits you earn overseas need to be acceptable for matriculation to schools in other countries as well. Ask to have copies of all required records and immunizations sent to your new school. More to evaluate schools can be found on page 31 in "CHECKLIST FOR A NEW SCHOOL."

In addition to academic considerations, other points to check are the environment and atmosphere of each school's campus, as well as the interaction between teachers and the student body. It is just as important to feel comfortable emotionally as it is academically. A change that is too drastic can impede your progress in the new country. Following is a case in point.

When we moved to England, one of my children was in the eleventh grade and planning for college. We were not well-informed about local schools and his first overseas educational experience was a drastic change from his former schooling. The change in study expectations and activities set in an entirely different environment delayed his adjustment to life overseas. The following semester we enrolled him in an "American School" nearby where the transition, atmosphere and overall experience made a positive impact on him. Immersion in an environment with which he was more familiar helped him to excel educationally and personally. This is just one reason why I believe that school research is a vital part of overseas education.

LOOKING TOWARD COLLEGE

If you are nearing the time to apply to college, ask how the international school handles standardized testing and procedures for college applications. The College Board advises American applicants returning home (for college) to begin the process as early as 18 months in advance. Almost every college makes information available on the Internet that applicants can review from anywhere in the world (search under the college name). If you will be attending one of the secondary "American Schools" overseas, its staff will be familiar with students who move often

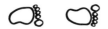

and will be knowledgeable about the issues and challenges of the application procedure for United States colleges.

BOARDING SCHOOLS

Boarding schools may be a common educational alternative in your new country. Carefully research this choice of education with your family. Just a few questions to ask include:

- daily regimen of the school,
- type of supervision,
- academic schedule,
- study requirements,
- meal schedule and diet,
- type of leisure activities,
- available transportation,
- supervision for on- and off-campus activities,
- amount of free time,
- amount of spending money required.

For students who have never lived away from home, a boarding school regimen and environment will be another change in lifestyle, in addition to the move to the new country.

OVERSEAS COLLEGES

If you are graduating from high school you may want to continue your studies in the country to which your family is moving. Studying abroad can be a unique experience, educationally and socially. If you choose this option, research the available courses as well as the atmosphere, instructors and schedule of the overseas universities. Understand how each school's degrees, programs and credits will be valued in your home country. Your hard-earned studies should be universally recognized, and therefore allow you to be competitive in various markets and in other parts of the world.

See also "EDUCATION" in the INTERNET DIRECTORY.

Although moving to another country involves learning new customs and possibly a new language, most of the suggestions outlined in SECTION ONE of this book will apply to your situation as well.

Recognize and express your feelings by keeping a journal, creating a scrapbook, using the "MEETING CHALLENGES" worksheets and sharing your thoughts and concerns with your family. This is especially important if you are struggling with a negative issue because each day with a dilemma can seem like an eternity.

It is essential that you reach out to make friends in your new city. Remember, the start to a great friendship could be as simple as walking up to someone with a smile on your face and saying "hello." If you are moving to a country where another language is spoken, learn a few phrases or conversation starters and practice using them.

Keep an even balance between doing activities that you have always enjoyed (i.e., sports, family celebrations) and trying new pastimes (foods, music, etc.). Make every moment count. And —think about how you want people to remember you as you leave your footsteps around the world!

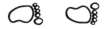

*"If a man does not keep pace with his companions,
perhaps it is because he hears a different drummer."*
—Henry D. Thoreau

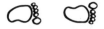

Exit Right-Enter Right By Dr. David Pollock

Re-entry! A word that entered the American vocabulary from the early days of the space program. Initially it addressed the issue of how to get man and machine back to the earth's surface safely. Within the last two decades it has taken on other meanings, as business people from all over the world relocate their families to other countries. After the assignment is over, they must all be prepared for re-entry into their "home" countries. Let's look at the following scenario.

Emmanuel moves from a Chicago suburb to Tokyo where he lives for three years while attending the American School in Japan. Japan is modern, the school is "American." US music, movies, sports and style are part of the general information available. Though Emmanuel enjoys Japan, he looks forward to returning to Chicago and his old friends.

When Emmanuel attempts to settle back into Chicago, however, he feels dissatisfied, disappointed and maybe even depressed. He misses sights and smells and sounds. He longs for the friends with whom he shared his Japanese experiences. He remembers good things and very few bad ones. The worst of it is the thoughts and feelings of regret he experiences, some specific, but most vague and nagging.

What's wrong? To put it simply, if you don't leave right you don't enter (or re-enter) right. Leaving right requires the individual to build a RAFT out of four critical actions.

R-Reconciliation

Failure to resolve conflict is like carrying an invisible backpack filled with very heavy trash. The "trash" may be people's guilt for things they have done to injure someone else. For this they need to seek forgiveness and then begin to rebuild the relationship. For others the "trash" may be bitterness because of something done to them or not done for them. In either case, reconciliation starts when we either seek forgiveness or give forgiveness.

Reconciliation is doing whatever is necessary to heal broken relationships *before you leave.*

A-Affirmation

This is the task (sometimes difficult) of letting others know you appreciate them. Affirmation is saying "thank you," "I'm glad we have been friends," "you are a special and important person to me," "I want to stay in contact with you" and maybe even "I love you." Say it, write it, give a gift and act in a way that communicates this. These actions not only free us to leave, but help others to let go *and* sets the stage for a warm, pleasant return.

F-Farewells

Don't just walk (or fly) away. Say good-bye in culturally appropriate ways to people who are important to you—and to whom you are important. Make a list of people to whom you should say good-bye and consider what kind of a "good-bye" it should be. Who do you say hello to everyday? Who have been your care givers? Who have you cared for? Should you have a meal with them? Should you drink "chai" (tea) or go for a walk together? Is a "good-bye" enough?

You need to say farewell to people, pets, places and possessions that you can't carry with you. Closure is important.

T-Think destination

Where are you going and what are your expectations? What will it be like when you arrive? Who will meet you? What will they be like? What will happen the first day, the first week, the first month? Write down what your mind pictures are and then share them with others who can help you evaluate them.

Life doesn't always go the way we want it, so your expectations need to be realistic. But they need to be positive too. After all, everything doesn't go wrong and even when something does, we usually have the resources and strength to solve the problem. By reconciling conflicts, affirming our friendships, saying our farewells and thinking positively and realistically about our new destination, we can leave right and open the way to enter right.

Dr. David Pollock, 1939-2004. David was co-founder and director of Interaction International, Incorporated. He was a resource and catalyst in the area of youth and family care and service since the early 1960s. David traveled extensively on every continent to conduct pre-experience and re-entry programs for adults and young people particularly in overseas assignments. He also co-authored The Third Culture Kids: The Experience of Growing Up Among Worlds, *with Ruth Van Reken. Dr. Pollock served on the faculty of Houghton College as Director of Intercultural Programs (1986-1992) and as an adjunct sociology instructor in intercultural studies (1986-2004). BR Anchor Publishing is honored to include Dr. Pollack's recognized RAFT theory in* Footsteps Around the World.

"There is no pleasure comparable to that of meeting an old friend, except the possibility of making a new one."
—René Descartes

79

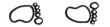

Notes

Crisscross Puzzle

Across

5. When meeting someone you should have a firm _____
8. present
10. eating a meal
11. lose one's temper
14. something to chew
15. sneakers cover these
17. you see with your _____
18. compensate; reimburse

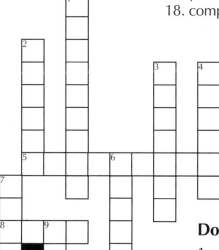

Down

1. illegally disposing trash
2. place of worship
3. clap for a job well done
4. third meal of the day
6. looking without blinking
7. supports your torso
9. teasing behavior
12. senior citizens
13. wait in line
16. shortest hand appendage

The answers are on page 92.

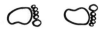

It's very tempting while living abroad to concentrate only on your life there, and not pay much attention to what is happening at home. However, you and your family will have home leave visits while living abroad and during these trips it is important to stay connected with people and events there. Note changes that are taking place in your home country and be aware of what your peers are wearing, saying, eating and doing for fun. It will be just as important when you move home to comfortably fit into that environment as it was to adapt to the one in the foreign country.

Lay the groundwork

☐ Discuss your hopes and expectations about moving home with family, friends and teachers.

☐ Think about the positive aspects of moving home: having more contact with grandparents, visiting favorite theme parks or doing the pastimes that you previously enjoyed.

☐ Plan how you will maintain friendships with people you met abroad.

☐ Learn as much as possible about the city to which you are moving. (Even if you are moving back to the same city, don't assume it will be the same.)

☐ If you are returning to the same community, ask a friend to spread the word that you are moving back and looking forward to being with them.

☐ Stay close to your family and have weekly family meetings to discuss what each of you can do to help smooth each other's transition.

☐ If you were involved in volunteer efforts overseas, ask for recommendation letters from teachers and organization sponsors for future volunteer efforts.

Gather mementos of places and experiences that you have had overseas. When you move back home you can use memorabilia from your travels along with pennants or other articles from your new school and community to decorate your bedroom.

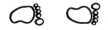

Assess Your Experience

As you near the time to repatriate, think about what helped you settle in overseas. Assess the personality traits, skills and attitudes that you believe were useful in adjusting to the foreign culture. A good exercise would be to answer the following questions.

What can I do now that I could not do before moving abroad?

_____

_____

How did I manage to overcome problems?

_____

_____

What personal accomplishments did I gain overseas?

_____

_____

How can I best use my new skills? _____

_____

_____

How did I relate to people in the host country?

_____

_____

How did I learn to adapt?

_____

_____

What safety precautions did I use?

_____

_____

After answering these questions, think about how you can incorporate these traits and experiences into your life back home.

HOME AGAIN

During repatriation, it is not unusual to experience a sense of loss for sights, sounds, customs and peoples. It will help if you stay in contact with former friends, as well as integrate into the new community. When you encounter situations that you once considered routine, but which now cause you emotional havoc, know that you are not alone. This is one more symptom of repatriation shock, and the strangeness you feel will pass.

When we repatriated to America after living in England, we moved back to the same community. We quickly learned that although our friends enjoyed hearing about our travels during our brief visits home, they no longer wanted to hear about all the wonderful places we had been overseas once we were living in the same small town. It was difficult because we felt uncomfortable talking about what had become our life for four years.

If you move back to the same city, take it slowly and prepare to rebuild friendships. It is seldom possible to simply pick up where one leaves off. And remember, if no one else wants to hear your stories, grandparents and relatives will lend a listening ear about life and activities abroad.

Do's and Don'ts

What you should do

- ❏ Network with other families who have lived overseas and share your thoughts with them about moving back. This association will provide support and allow you to discuss your feelings about adjusting to a new school and community, in addition to suggesting ways to work through the repatriation process.
- ❏ Ask new acquaintances about their lives, city and activities.
- ❏ Find activities and clubs where you can use the skills that you learned from living in a multicultural environment.
- ❏ If you have younger brothers and sisters, see what you can do to help them through the change. Reaching out to others can take your mind off your own challenges.
- ❏ Volunteer your time and talent to a worthwhile organization.
- ❏ Assist other expatriates as they relocate to your country.
- ❏ Join or create a welcome club in your new school. See also "Welcome Clubs" on page 50.
- ❏ Seek out exchange students because you may have a lot in common with them.
- ❏ Join a language club at school.
- ❏ Investigate student internship opportunities at local companies that have a global focus.
- ❏ Keep a journal of your feelings and activities.

Become involved in your new community and think about ways you can put your experiences to use in a positive manner.

What not to do

- ❏ Overdose friends with excerpts of trips and travels in other countries.
- ❏ Make comparisons between the home country and the one you left, or between old and new friends and schools.

❐ Blame others for challenges you are experiencing. Keep in mind the reasons why you and your family are moving home and how this transition can ultimately benefit each of you.

❐ Lose track of former friends. It is important to make new friends, but maintain contact with others you met.

❐ Hesitate to take advantage of counseling assistance if you are struggling. A few sessions with a counselor may help you through an otherwise drawn-out and uncomfortable situation.

❐ Be too concerned if you adjust to the new lifestyle more slowly than other members of your family. Everyone adapts at different speeds and in different ways.

MAKE YOUR EXPERIENCE COUNT

As a repatriated individual, your acquired perspective, knowledge and experience will be invaluable. Offer to share what you have learned about the country in which you lived with schools, clubs or organizations. A few suggestions that you can use in a discussion are:

🦶 living conditions,

🦶 culture and what makes it unique,

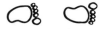

- availability (or non-existence) of products and services that you were accustomed to in your home country,

- language skills necessary to function on a daily basis,

- how you found resources to help you in your transition.

You should also mention personal characteristics and attitudes that you had, or developed, that were helpful in achieving a successful overseas experience.

People who have lived in other countries usually find that they have become more curious and adaptable, and interface more easily with new acquaintances. Keep in mind that you will need time to readjust and that all of the experiences you gained, both wonderful and challenging, will make a difference in you as a person and will benefit you for the rest of your life.

Section Three

3 Resources

Double Puzzle - page 45

1	test	7	year	13	traffic lights
2	laws	8	serviced	14	mechanic
3	insurance	9	mileage	15	stop signs
4	registration	10	tires rotated	16	defensive
5	license	11	oil filter		
6	model	12	road signs		

Driving Phrase: PRACTICE SAFE DRIVING

International Road Signs - page 70

1	railroad crossing	7	slippery road ahead
2	pedestrian crosswalk	8	traffic circle area
3	caution: bicycles	9	gas & diesel station
4	road narrows	10	no fires allowed
5	children at play	11	biochemical hazard
6	no horseback riding	12	credit cards not accepted

Customs And Manners Quiz - page 71

1	Belgium	8	Hong Kong	15	India
2	England	9	Netherlands	16	New Zealand
3	Germany	10	Italy	17	Pakistan
4	China	11	Jordan	18	Singapore
5	Japan	12	South Africa	19	Colombia
6	Mexico	13	Saudi Arabia	20	Japan
7	Saudi Arabia	14	China		

Crisscross Puzzle - page 81

Across

5	handshake	17	eyes	6	staring
8	gift	18	pay	7	legs
10	dining	**Down**		9	flirtatious
11	anger	1	littering	12	elderly
14	gum	2	church	13	queue
15	feet	3	applaud	16	thumb
		4	dinner		

E-mail Addresses

NAME _____

E-MAIL ADDRESS _____

MEMO _____

NAME _____

E-MAIL ADDRESS _____

MEMO _____

NAME _____

E-MAIL ADDRESS _____

MEMO _____

NAME _____

E-MAIL ADDRESS _____

MEMO _____

NAME _____

E-MAIL ADDRESS _____

MEMO _____

NAME _____

E-MAIL ADDRESS _____

MEMO _____

E-mail Addresses

NAME _____

E-MAIL ADDRESS _____

MEMO _____

NAME _____

E-MAIL ADDRESS _____

MEMO _____

NAME _____

E-MAIL ADDRESS _____

MEMO _____

NAME _____

E-MAIL ADDRESS _____

MEMO _____

NAME _____

E-MAIL ADDRESS _____

MEMO _____

NAME _____

E-MAIL ADDRESS _____

MEMO _____

Message From the Publisher

MESSAGE FROM THE PUBLISHER

*The Internet sites listed in the following
section were reviewed by our staff and
found to be helpful resources,
not only for your move but for your
homework assignments as well.*

*Please take the time to read "INTERNET SAFETY"
on the next page before you begin.*

Internet Safety

Internet sites, although accurate at the time this book went to press, are subject to change without notice.

BR Anchor Publishing recommends that when visiting Internet chat rooms, you

- ❐ do not submit your name, address, telephone number or school name (this applies to any Internet site as well);
- ❐ do not call anyone collect because your telephone number will appear on their bill;
- ❐ are careful of what you say;
- ❐ realize that if something sounds too good to be true, it probably is;
- ❐ are wary of someone who asks you too much too soon;
- ❐ are not afraid to say you will get back to a person later about a question that you do not like (then discuss the question with a parent, guardian or friend);
- ❐ terminate the conversation if someone with whom you are talking is extremely evasive.

Internet Directory

CITY/COUNTRY INFORMATION

Chamber of Commerce www.chamber-of-commerce.com
This website includes over 20,000 US city guides and international chamber of commerce listings. Search this directory for city listings all around the world.

Cities.com www.cities.com Search the database of 4,329 city guides in 150 different countries. Extensive information, links to local attractions and top news stories.

International Newspaper Links www.nettizen.com/newspaper
Comprehensive searchable resource for 3,400 worldwide newspaper and magazine links to read local news about your new city.

WorldAtlas.com www.worldatlas.com A large assortment of world maps (with various views), a large selection of country flags, local country time, geography questions (they supply answers and useful links) and map clip art that can be used at no charge.

You can also input your new city, state and/or country (e.g., "Spokane and Washington" or "Rome and Italy") in any search engine to learn about the area's recreation facilities, customs/trends, culture, languages and useful expressions.

EDUCATION

CollegeNET www.collegenet.com Quickly find the ideal college. Narrow choices by region, sports, major, tuition and several other criteria. Hotlink from your search directly to home pages of the schools in which you are interested. Review, compare and sort schools according to exclusive, detailed profiles.

CollegeView www.collegeview.com Free online service to search for all accredited colleges and universities in the United States and Canada. Tours of hundreds of schools, electronic college applications, scholarships, financial aid and career information.

European Council of International Schools (ECIS) www.ecis.org
The largest association of international schools that features *The International Schools Directory* and Higher Education Institutions.

International Schools Services (ISS) www.iss.edu The *ISS Directory of Overseas Schools* is a comprehensive guide to K-12 American and international schools.

Mapping Your Future www.mapping-your-future.org Provides information about higher education and career opportunities. This site also offers online student loan counseling.

The Princeton Review www.princetonreview.com Standardized test preparation: courses, books, software and online services. Small classes, personal attention, a unique approach and great results are some key characteristics. Students can gather information about tests, admissions, internships and career programs, as well as a broad range of basic skill-building courses and professional and career programs.

You can also use web search engines by entering the school name and city such as "Central High and Cleveland" to view photos, school calendars, publications, courses, sports and more.

FINANCES

Consumer Education for Teens www.wa.gov/ago/teenconsumer
Don't miss this site! Learn how to avoid being the victim of various types of fraud, from music clubs and calling cards to Internet scams and get-rich-quick schemes.

My Future www.myfuture.com My Future has lots of great information about financial aid, scholarships and careers, getting great jobs and managing your money.

The Young Investor www.younginvestor.com Liberty Financial's Young Investor Web Site, a place to learn about money and maybe even earn some too.

PART-TIME EMPLOYMENT

Gotajob.com www.gotajob.com Part-Time. In No Time. This exciting FREE Internet service is designed to match individuals seeking hourly work with potential employers. This new service is perfect for high school and college students.

Safe Sitter® www.safesitter.org This site teaches adolescent babysitters how to handle crises, keep their charges secure and nurture and guide young children.

SummerJobs.com www.summerjobs.com This site features summer job opportunities for students and temporary workers. Links to: OverseasJobs.com, ResortJobs.com, InternJobs.com and more.

teens4hire www.teens4hire.org This site has been recognized in *USA Today, The Wall Street Journal*, on NBC, CBS and more.

Teens 14 and older can search jobs, apply online, be considered for job openings and receive the latest news and information on teen employment.

MILITARY SITES

Armed Services YMCA www.asymca.org Look here for information and links to our 18 branches and other program sites, including those run by community YMCAs and the Defense Department.

DoDEA for Teens www.odedodea.edu/teens The Department of Defense Education Activity page for teens provides information about all DoDEA schools, registration, scholarship opportunities, college planning and more.

Military Teens on the Move www.dod.mil/mtom This site offers great information about Making the Move, Youth Sponsorship, DoDDS and Civilian schools, links to installation websites and more.

Standard Installation Topic Exchange Service (SITES) www.dmdc.osd.mil/sites Worldwide relocation assistance for major military installations. For all branches of military personnel and their families. Requires a military ID number and date of birth to enter. If you have problems accessing this site, contact your base relocation department for assistance.

INTERNATIONAL INFORMATION

Berlitz International, Inc. www.berlitz.com Language and cross-cultural training programs and interpretation services, as well as self-teaching and language reference materials, phrase books, dictionaries and travel guides.

Interaction International, Inc. www.tckinteract.net Its primary focus is the care of MKs and TCKs and their families. Resources, seminars and *Among Worlds,* a quarterly magazine for missionary, military, diplomat and business expat teens. A catalyst and resource for the family, church and missions community.

The Web of Culture www.webofculture.com A wealth of information relating to cross-cultural communications. This site informs its audience about the people and cultures of the world covering world capitals, news headlines, body language and much more.

travlang www.travlang.com Hosts Foreign Languages for Travelers pages which teach the basics of over 900 languages and includes translating dictionaries. travlang also links to multilingual bookstores, language schools, translating services and general travel resources.

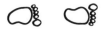

World Association of Girl Guides and Girl Scouts
www.wagggsworld.org Provides girls and young women with
excellent training and programmes addressing their intellectual, spiritual,
mental and physical needs. WAGGGS' Mission is to enable girls and
young women to develop their fullest potential as responsible citizens
of the world.

Youth For Understanding (YFU) www.yfu.org A non-profit educational
organization which offers opportunities for young people around the
world to spend a summer, semester or year with a host family in
another country.

SCOUTING

Boy Scouts of America www.scouting.org Provides an educational
program for boys ages 7-20 to build character, train in the responsibilities
of participating in citizenship and develop personal fitness. Parents
might be interested in being a Scout leader.

Girl Scouts of the USA www.girlscouts.org The world's preeminent
organization dedicated solely to girls ages 5-17. In Girl Scouts, girls
discover the fun, friendship and power of girls together. Girl Scouts
welcomes adult volunteer participation.

VOLUNTEER EFFORTS

Cool Works www.coolworks.com/showme/vlnteer.htm Gain access to
a number of volunteer organizations, including Global Volunteers,
The Student Conservation Association and Habitat for Humanity.

SERVEnet www.servenet.org The World of Service and Volunteering tells
how volunteering your time and talents can benefit you.

VolunteerMatch www.volunteermatch.org Search by your zip code and
city to select an organization, use the non-profit directory and check
out the virtual volunteer opportunities.

Youth Service America (YSA) www.ysa.org A resource center and the
premier alliance of over 200 organizations committed to increasing the
quantity and quality of opportunities for young Americans to serve
locally, nationally or globally.

OTHER RELEVANT SITES

BBC NEWS www.bbc.co.uk News in English, replay of the BBC Television's Nine O'clock News and BBC radio broadcasts.

BR Anchor Publishing www.branchor.com Chat anywhere around the world with your friends using our secure online chat room and test your knowledge of other cultures using our culture quiz.

National Geographic www.nationalgeographic.com Learn about the world, enjoy fun games and select a pen-pal.

National Public Radio www.npr.org Transcripts are available for programs such as: *Morning Edition, All Things Considered, Car Talk* and *Talk of the Nation.*

Passport information www.travel.state.gov/passport_services.html Application process (e.g., fees, locations, forms and status inquiries) plus passport related news.

ShyKids.com www.shykids.com This website discusses shyness: what it feels like, what it looks like and most importantly, how to feel more comfortable with who you are and who you are with.

Travel Warnings www.travel.state.gov Lists the United States Embassy and Consulate locations, minor political disturbances, health conditions, crime and security information and drug penalties for every country of the world.

Young Life www.younglife.com For teenagers everywhere. Young Life provides healthy, creative fun while instilling excellent values. From weekly clubs to seasonal camping experiences to daily outings with leaders, Young Life is known around the world as the organization that knows how to have fun.

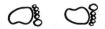

Books in Print

Let's Make A Move! This well-reviewed book helps young children who are moving within, or inpatriating to, the United States. It is designed to help children become more confident, express their feelings about moving and learn rules to keep them safe, as well as learn about their new city. Includes two sticker pages.

Let's Move Overseas contains all the creative activities, ideas and fun stickers that made *Let's Make A Move!* so successful. However, it specifically addresses international concerns such as culture, language and safety that help children adjust to a foreign country.

The League of Super Movers A unique book for 9-12 year olds. The League of Super Movers are characters who guide John and Michelle on an exciting moving adventure. The story line and puzzles in this full-color book provide moving advice, safety tips and methods to learn about the new home.

Footsteps Around the World This unique book has everything teenagers need to move—and then some. Advice to organize a move, make new friends, stay safe and realize a positive relocation experience. This comprehensive book includes checklists and over 40 helpful Internet resources.

Relocation 101 Domestic
Home Away From Home International

These books address professional and family challenges that impede relocation success. Topics include: two career families; children and education; home sales and purchases; financial, insurance and medical concerns; elder care issues; organizing a move and much more. Each book contains more than 60 valuable Internet resources and time-tested checklists.

You can read excerpts and book reviews about all of these books at www.branchor.com. Personalized books are a BR Anchor Publishing specialty. To see examples of custom and translated books, visit www.branchor.com/custombooks.htm.